Pip's
Mess

by Alison Hawes
Illustrated by Bill Ledger

OXFORD
UNIVERSITY PRESS

In this story ...

Pip

Pip can pick up rocks.

Mrs Molten

Slink

2

Pip is in the lab.

Add six drops of liquid.

Pip trips.
She adds *lots* of liquid!

The liquid fizzes.

It runs on to the desk.

The liquid drips on Slink.

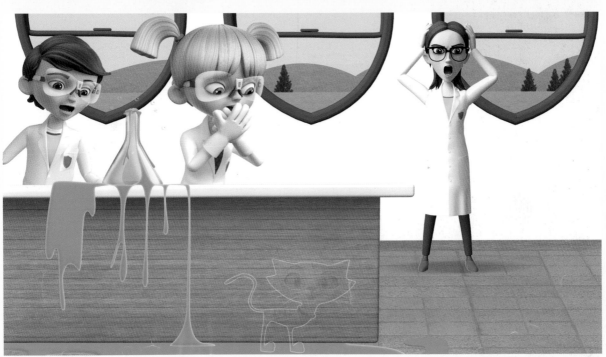

Pip cannot stop the liquid.
Pip yells.

Quick!

The liquid stops.

zip

Slink is back!

Pip is glad.

Slink is mad.

He hands Pip a mop.

Pip mops up the mess.

Retell the story ...

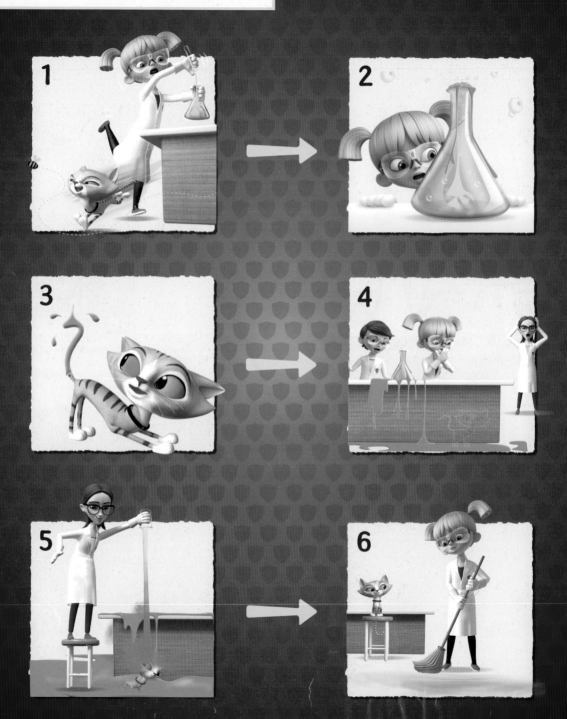